THE
ENCHIRIDION

THE ENCHIRIDION

A STOIC'S GUIDE TO CONTENTMENT AND TRANQUILITY

EPICTETUS

TRANSLATED BY
GEORGE LONG

ixia
PRESS

Garden City, New York

Bibliographical Note

This Ixia Press edition, first published in 2023, is an unabridged republication of the work first published by Dover Publications in 2004. The Dover edition was an unabridged republication of the *Encheiridion* and "Fragments" from *The Discourses of Epictetus, with the Encheiridion and Fragments*, originally published by A. L. Burt, Publisher, New York, n.d. A new Publisher's Note was specially prepared for that Dover edition. "Enchiridion," meaning manual, is sometimes transliterated as "Encheiridion."

Library of Congress Cataloging-in-Publication Data

Names: Epictetus, author. | Long, George, 1800–1879, translator.
Title: The Enchiridion : a Stoic's guide to contentment and tranquility / Epictetus ; translated by George Long.
Other titles: Manual. English
Description: Garden City, New York : Ixia Press, [2023] | "This Ixia Press edition, first published in 2023, is an unabridged republication of the work first published by Dover Publications in 2004. That Dover edition was an unabridged republication of the Encheiridion and 'Fragments' from The Discourses of Epictetus, with the Encheiridion and Fragments, originally published by A. L. Burt, Publisher, New York, n.d. A new Publisher's Note was specially prepared for that Dover edition." | Includes bibliographical references. | Summary: "Epictetus maintained that all people are free to control their lives and live in harmony with nature. This book offers practical guidelines for those seeking contentment and those who have already made some progress in that direction" —Provided by publisher.
Identifiers: LCCN 2023008328 | ISBN 9780486851952 | ISBN 0486851958
Subjects: LCSH: Ethics, Ancient. | Conduct of life—Early works to 1800.
Classification: LCC B561.M52 E5 2023 | DDC 180—dc23/eng/20230301
LC record available at https://lccn.loc.gov/2023008328

Ixia Press
An imprint of Dover Publications

Printed in China by Chang Jiang Printing Media Co., Ltd.
85195801   2023
www.doverpublications.com/ixiapress

Contents

Publisher's Note

The Stoic philosopher Epictetus was born ca. 50 CE in Hierapolis, Phrygia (southwestern Turkey). Little is known of his life other than that he was apparently lame and weak, was a slave as a boy in Rome, and subsequently became a freedman; and that he attended the lectures of the Stoic philosopher Musonius Rufus. In 90 CE Epictetus, along with other philosophers, was expelled from Rome by the Emperor Domitian, who was apparently angered by the Stoic philosophers' support of his opponents. Epictetus spent the rest of his life at Nicopolis in southern Epirus (Greece).

Epictetus wrote no works of his own; instead, his discourses were recorded by a disciple, Arrian, who preserved them for posterity. The philosopher's teachings are disposed in two formats: the *Discourses,* of which four books have survived; and the *Encheiridion,* or Manual, a shorter aphoristic version of the principal themes of the *Discourses.* Although Stoic philosophy dealt with other disciplines, such as logic and physics, the works of Epictetus focus almost exclusively on ethics. Like other moral philosophers, his aim is to show people how to lead better lives, i.e., to achieve *eudaimonia* ("happiness" or "flourishing"). For Epictetus, the way to do this is by living a virtuous life. Only virtue or virtuous activities are good, and the only evil is vice, or actions motivated by vice.

In the Stoic view, our capacity to be happy is completely dependent on ourselves—how we treat ourselves, how we relate to others, and how we react to events in general. Events are good or bad only in terms of our reaction to them. We must not try to predict or control what happens, but merely to accept events with equanimity. The only thing we control is our will, and God has given us a will that cannot be influenced or thwarted by external events—unless we allow it. We are not responsible for the ideas or events that present themselves to us, but only for the ways in which we act on them.

The teaching of Epictetus suggests that man should be grateful to God for all things, and should be content with whatever occurs, for whatever happens is God's will, and the deity's choice is bound to be superior to human wishes. "God" in this case is not the divine being of Judaeo-Christian theology, but a material immanence conceived of as a fiery breath infused in all things. This force of nature creates and directs the world as we experience it and it is therefore up to the individual to live according to nature, since this divine intelligence has made the best of all possible worlds. (Not surprisingly, the religious tone of Epictetus' thought recommended him to many early Christian thinkers.).

Epictetus was considered the greatest of the Stoic philosophers by Herodes Atticus, a teacher of Marcus Aurelius, while Origen, one of the early Church fathers, asserted that Epictetus was more popular in his own day than Plato was in his. This volume offers a concise cross-section of the philosopher's work suggesting the reasons for that eminence and popularity.

It also attests to the enduring power of the Stoic ethos, as well as providing insight into the thought of one of the most influential Greek thinkers of the first and second centuries.

THE ENCHEIRIDION, OR MANUAL

I.

Of things some are in our power, and others are not. In our power are opinion, movement toward a thing, desire, aversion (turning from a thing); and in a word, whatever are our own acts: not in our power are the body, property, reputation, offices (magisterial power), and in a word, whatever are not our own acts. And the things in our power are by nature free, not subject to restraint nor hindrance: but the things not in our power are weak, slavish, subject to restraint, in the power of others. Remember then that if you think the things which are by nature slavish to be free, and the things which are in the power of others to be your own, you will be hindered, you will lament, you will be disturbed, you will blame both gods and men: but if you think that only which is your own to be your own, and if you think that what is another's, as it really is, belongs to another, no man will ever compel you, no man will hinder you, you will never blame any man, you will accuse no man, you will do nothing involuntarily (against your will), no man will harm you, you will have no enemy, for you will not suffer any harm.

If then you desire (aim at) such great things, remember that you must not (attempt to) lay hold of them with a small effort; but you must leave alone some things entirely, and postpone others for the present. But if you wish for these things also (such great things), and power (office) and wealth, perhaps you will not gain even these very things (power and wealth) because you aim also at those former things (such great things): certainly you will fail in those things through which alone happiness and freedom are secured. Straightway then practice saying to every harsh appearance,[1] You are an appearance, and in no manner what you appear to be. Then examine it by the rules which you possess, and by this first and chiefly, whether it relates to the things which are in our power or to the things which are not in our power: and if it relates to anything which is not in our power, be ready to say, that it does not concern you.

II.

Remember that desire contains in it the profession (hope) of obtaining that which you desire; and the profession (hope) in aversion (turning from a thing) is that you will not fall into that which you attempt to avoid: and he who fails in his desire is unfortunate; and he who falls into that which he would avoid, is unhappy. If then you attempt to avoid only the things contrary to nature which are within your power, you will not be involved in any of the things which you would avoid. But if you attempt to avoid disease or death or poverty, you will be unhappy. Take away then aversion from all things which are not in our power, and transfer it to the things contrary to nature which are in our power. But destroy desire completely for the present. For if you desire anything which is not in our power, you must be unfortunate: but of the things in our power, and which it would be good to desire, nothing yet is before you. But employ only the power of moving toward an object and retiring from it; and these powers indeed only slightly and with exceptions and with remission.

III.

In everything which pleases the soul, or supplies a want, or is loved, remember to add this to the (description, notion); what is the nature of each thing, beginning from the smallest? If you love an earthen vessel, say it is an earthen vessel which you love; for when it has been broken, you will not be disturbed. If you are kissing your child or wife, say that it is a human being whom you are kissing, for when the wife or child dies, you will not be disturbed.

IV.

When you are going to take in hand any act, remind yourself what kind of an act it is. If you are going to bathe, place before yourself what happens in the bath: some splashing the water, others pushing against one another, others abusing one another, and some stealing: and thus with more safety you will undertake the matter, if you say to yourself, I now intend to bathe, and to maintain my will in a manner conformable to nature. And so you will do in every act: for thus if any hindrance to bathing shall happen, let this thought be ready; it was not this only that I intended, but I intended also to maintain my will in a way conformable to nature; but I shall not maintain it so, if I am vexed at what happens.

V.

Men are disturbed not by the things which happen, but by the opinions about the things: for example, death is nothing terrible, for if it were, it would have seemed so to Socrates; for the opinion about death, that it is terrible, is the terrible thing. When then we are impeded or disturbed or grieved, let us never blame others, but ourselves, that is, our opinions. It is the act of an ill-instructed man to blame others for his own bad condition; it is the act of one who has begun to be instructed, to lay the blame on himself; and of one whose instruction is completed, neither to blame another, nor himself.

VI.

Be not elated at any advantage (excellence), which belongs to another. If a horse when he is elated should say, I am beautiful, one might endure it. But when you are elated, and say, I have a beautiful horse, you must know that you are elated at having a good horse.[2] What then is your own? The use of appearances. Consequently when in the use of appearances you are conformable to nature, then be elated, for then you will be elated at something good which is your own.

VII.

As on a voyage when the vessel has reached a port, if you go out to get water, it is an amusement by the way to pick up a shell-fish or some bulb, but your thoughts ought to be directed to the ship, and you ought to be constantly watching if the captain should call, and then you must throw away all those things, that you may not be bound and pitched into the ship like sheep: so in life also, if there be given to you instead of a little bulb and a shell a wife and child, there will be nothing to prevent (you from taking them). But if the captain should call, run to the ship, and leave all those things without regard to them. But if you are old, do not even go far from the ship, lest when you are called you make default.

VIII.

Seek not that the things which happen should happen as you wish; but wish the things which happen to be as they are, and you will have a tranquil flow of life.

IX.

Disease is an impediment to the body, but not to the will, unless the will itself chooses. Lameness is an impediment to the leg, but not to the will. And add this reflection on the occasion of everything that happens; for you will find it an impediment to something else, but not to yourself.

X.

On the occasion of every accident (event) that befalls you, remember to turn to yourself and inquire what power you have for turning it to use. If you see a fair man or a fair woman, you will find that the power to resist is temperance (continence). If labor (pain) be presented to you, you will find that it is endurance. If it be abusive words, you will find it to be patience. And if you have been thus formed to the (proper) habit, the appearances will not carry you along with them.

XI.

Never say about anything, I have lost it, but say I have restored it. Is your child dead? It has been restored. Is your wife dead? She has been restored. Has your estate been taken from you? Has not then this also been restored? But he who has taken it from me is a bad man. But what is it to you, by whose hands the giver demanded it back? So long as he may allow you, take care of it as a thing which belongs to another, as travelers do with their inn.

XII.

If you intend to improve, throw away such thoughts as these: if I neglect my affairs, I shall not have the means of living: unless I chastise my slave, he will be bad. For it is better to die of hunger and so to be released from grief and fear than to live in abundance with perturbation; and it is better for your slave to be bad than for you to be unhappy.[3] Begin then from little things. Is the oil spilled? Is a little wine stolen? Say on the occasion, at such price is sold freedom from perturbation; at such price is sold tranquillity, but nothing is got for nothing. And when you call your slave, consider that it is possible that he does not hear; and if he does hear, that he will do nothing which you wish. But matters are not so well with him, but altogether well with you, that it should be in his power for you to be not disturbed.[4]

XIII.

If you would improve, submit to be considered without sense and foolish with respect to externals. Wish to be considered to know nothing: and if you shall seem to some to be a person of importance, distrust yourself. For you should know that it is not easy both to keep your will in a condition conformable to nature and (to secure) external things: but if a man is careful about the one, it is an absolute necessity that he will neglect the other.

XIV.

If you would have your children and your wife and your friends to live forever, you are silly; for you would have the things which are not in your power to be in your power, and the things which belong to others to be yours. So if you would have your slave to be free from faults, you are a fool; for you would have badness not to be badness, but something else.[5] But if you wish not to fail in your desires, you are able to do that. Practice then this which you are able to do. He is the master of every man who has the power over the things, which another person wishes or does not wish, the power to confer them on him or to take them away. Whoever then wishes to be free, let him neither wish for anything nor avoid anything which depends on others: if he does not observe this rule, he must be a slave.

XV.

Remember that in life you ought to behave as at a banquet. Suppose that something is carried round and is opposite to you. Stretch out your hand and take a portion with decency. Suppose that it passes by you. Do not detain it. Suppose that it is not yet come to you. Do not send your desire forward to it, but wait till it is opposite to you. Do so with respect to children, so with respect to a wife, so with respect to magisterial offices, so with respect to wealth, and you will be some time a worthy partner of the banquets of the gods. But if you take none of the things which are set before you, and even despise them, then you will be not only a fellow-banqueter with the gods, but also a partner with them in power. For by acting thus Diogenes and Heracleitus and those like them were deservedly divine, and were so called.

XVI.

When you see a person weeping in sorrow either when a child goes abroad or when he is dead, or when the man has lost his property, take care that the appearance do not hurry you away with it, as if he were suffering in external things.[6] But straightway make a distinction in your own mind, and be in readiness to say, it is not that which has happened that afflicts this man, for it does not afflict another, but it is the opinion about this thing which afflicts the man. So far as words then do not be unwilling to show him sympathy,[7] and even if it happens so, to lament with him. But take care that you do not lament internally also.

XVII.

Remember that thou art an actor in a play of such a kind as the teacher (author) may choose; if short, of a short one; if long, of a long one: if he wishes you to act the part of a poor man, see that you act the part naturally; if the part of a lame man, of a magistrate, of a private person, (do the same). For this is your duty, to act well the part that is given to you; but to select the part, belongs to another.

XVIII.

When a raven has croaked inauspiciously, let not the appearance hurry you away with it; but straightway make a distinction in your mind and say, None of these things is signified to me, but either to my poor body, or to my small property, or to my reputation, or to my children or to my wife: but to me all significations are auspicious if I choose. For whatever of these things results, it is in my power to derive benefit from it.

XIX.

You can be invincible, if you enter into no contest in which it is not in your power to conquer. Take care then when you observe a man honored before others or possessed of great power or highly esteemed for any reason, not to suppose him happy, and be not carried away by the appearance. For if the nature of the good is in our power, neither envy nor jealousy will have a place in us. But you yourself will not wish to be a general or senator or consul, but a free man: and there is only one way to this, to despise (care not for) the things which are not in our power.

XX.

Remember that it is not he who reviles you or strikes you, who insults you, but it is your opinion about these things as being insulting. When then a man irritates you, you must know that it is your own opinion which has irritated you. Therefore especially try not to be carried away by the appearance. For if you once gain time and delay, you will more easily master yourself.

XXI.

Let death and exile and every other thing which appears dreadful be daily before your eyes; but most of all death: and you will never think of anything mean nor will you desire anything extravagantly.

XXII.

If you desire philosophy, prepare yourself from the beginning to be ridiculed, to expect that many will sneer at you, and say, He has all at once returned to us as a philosopher; and whence does he get this supercilious look for us? Do you not show a supercilious look; but hold on to the things which seem to you best as one appointed by God to this station. And remember that if you abide in the same principles, these men who first ridiculed will afterward admire you: but if you shall have been overpowered by them, you will bring on yourself double ridicule.

XXIII.

If it should ever happen to you to be turned to externals in order to please some person, you must know that you have lost your purpose in life.[8] Be satisfied then in everything with being a philosopher; and if you wish to seem also to any person to be a philosopher, appear so to yourself, and you will be able to do this.

XXIV.

Let not these thoughts afflict you, I shall live unhonored and be nobody nowhere. For if want of honor (ἀτιμία) is an evil, you cannot be in evil through the means (fault) of another any more than you can be involved in anything base. Is it then your business to obtain the rank of a magistrate, or to be received at a banquet? By no means. How then can this be want of honor (dishonor)? And how will you be nobody nowhere, when you ought to be somebody in those things only which are in your power, in which indeed it is permitted to you to be a man of the greatest worth? But your friends will be without assistance! What do you mean by being without assistance? They will not receive money from you, nor will you make them Roman citizens. Who then told you that these are among the things which are in our power, and not in the power of others? And who can give to another what he has not himself? Acquire money then, your friends say, that we also may have something. If I can acquire money and also keep myself modest, and faithful and magnanimous, point out the way, and I will acquire it. But if you ask me to lose the things which are good and my own, in order that you may gain the things which are not good, see how unfair and silly you are. Besides, which would you rather have, money or a faithful and modest friend? For this end then rather help me to be such a man, and do not ask me to do this by which I shall lose that character. But my country, you say, as far as it depends on me, will be without my help. I ask again, what help do you mean? It will not have porticoes or baths through you. And what does this mean? For it is not furnished with shoes by means of a smith, nor with arms by means of a shoemaker. But it is enough if every man fully discharges the work that is his own: and if you provided it with another citizen faithful and modest, would you not be useful to it? Yes. Then you also cannot be useless to it. What place then, you say, shall I hold in the city? Whatever you can, if you maintain at the same time your fidelity and modesty. But if when you wish to be useful to the state, you shall lose these qualities, what profit could you be to it, if you were made shameless and faithless?

XXV.

Has any man been preferred before you at a banquet, or in being saluted, or in being invited to a consultation? If these things are good, you ought to rejoice that he has obtained them: but if bad, be not grieved because you have not obtained them; and remember that you cannot, if you do not the same things in order to obtain what is not in our power, be considered worthy of the same (equal) things. For how can a man obtain an equal share with another when he does not visit a man's doors as that other man does, when he does not attend him when he goes abroad, as the other man does; when he does not praise (flatter) him as another does? You will be unjust then and insatiable, if you do not part with the price, in return for which those things are sold, and if you wish to obtain them for nothing. Well, what is the price of lettuces? An obolus[9] perhaps. If then a man gives up the obolus, and receives the lettuces, and if you do not give up the obolus and do not obtain the lettuces, do not suppose that you receive less than he who has got the lettuces; for as he has the lettuces, so you have the obolus which you did not give. In the same way then in the other matter also you have not been invited to a man's feast, for you did not give to the host the price at which the supper is sold; but he sells it for praise (flattery), he sells it for personal attention. Give then the price, if it is for your interest, for which it is sold. But if you wish both not to give the price and to obtain the things, you are insatiable and silly. Have you nothing then in place of the supper? You have indeed, you have the not flattering of him, whom you did not choose to flatter; you have the not enduring of the man when he enters the room.

XXVI.

We may learn the wish (will) of nature from the things in which we do not differ from one another; for instance, when your neighbor's slave has broken his cup, or anything else, we are ready to say forthwith, that it is one of the things which happen. You must know then that when your cup also is broken, you ought to think as you did when your neighbor's cup was broken. Transfer this reflection to greater things also. Is another man's child or wife dead? There is no one who would not say, this is an event incident to man. But when a man's own child or wife is dead, forthwith he calls out, Wo to me, how wretched I am. But we ought to remember how we feel when we hear that it has happened to others.

XXVII.

As a mark is not set up for the purpose of missing the aim, so neither does the nature of evil exist in the world.[10]

XXVIII.

If any person was intending to put your body in the power of any man whom you fell in with on the way, you would be vexed: but that you put your understanding in the power of any man whom you meet, so that if he should revile you, it is disturbed and troubled, are you not ashamed at this?

XXIX.[11]

In every act observe the things which come first, and those which follow it; and so proceed to the act. If you do not, at first you will approach it with alacrity, without having thought of the things which will follow; but afterward, when certain base (ugly) things have shown themselves, you will be ashamed. A man wishes to conquer at the Olympic games. I also wish indeed, for it is a fine thing. But observe both the things which come first, and the things which follow; and then begin the act. You must do everything according to rule, eat according to strict orders, abstain from delicacies, exercise yourself as you are bid at appointed times, in heat, in cold, you must not drink cold water, nor wine as you choose; in a word, you must deliver yourself up to the exercise master as you do to the physician, and then proceed to the contest. And sometimes you will strain the hand, put the ankle out of joint, swallow much dust, sometimes be flogged, and after all this be defeated. When you have considered all this, if you still choose, go to the contest: if you do not, you will behave like children, who at one time play at wrestlers, another time as flute players, again as gladiators, then as trumpeters, then as tragic actors: so you also will be at one time an athlete, at another a gladiator, then a rhetorician, then a philosopher, but with your whole soul you will be nothing at all; but like an ape you imitate everything that you see, and one thing after another pleases you. For you have not undertaken anything with consideration, nor have you surveyed it well; but carelessly and with cold desire. Thus some who have seen a philosopher and having heard one speak, as Euphrates speaks,—and who can speak as he does?—they wish to be philosophers themselves also. My man, first of all consider what kind of thing it is: and then examine your own nature, if you are able to sustain the character. Do you wish to be a pentathlete or a wrestler? Look at your arms, your thighs, examine your loins. For different men are formed by nature for different things. Do you think that if you do these things, you can eat in the same manner, drink in the same manner, and in the same manner loath certain things? You must pass sleepless nights, endure toil, go away from your kinsmen, be despised by a slave, in everything have the inferior part, in honor, in office, in the courts of justice, in every little matter. Consider these things, if you would exchange for them, freedom from passions, liberty, tranquillity. If not, take care that, like little children, you be not now a philosopher, then a servant of the publicani, then a rhetorician, then a procurator (manager) for Caesar. These things are not consistent. You must be one man, either good or bad. Yon must either cultivate your own ruling faculty, or external things; you must either exercise your skill on internal things or on external things; that is you must either maintain the position of a philosopher or that of a common person.

XXX.

Duties are universally measured by relations. Is a man a father? The precept is to take care of him, to yield to him in all things, to submit when he is reproachful, when he inflicts blows. But suppose that he is a bad father. Were you then by nature made akin to a good father? No; but to a father. Does a brother wrong you? Maintain then your own position toward him, and do not examine what he is doing, but what you must do that your will shall be conformable to nature. For another will not damage you, unless you choose: but you will be damaged then when you shall think that you are damaged. In this way then you will discover your duty from the relation of a neighbor, from that of a citizen, from that of a general, if you are accustomed to contemplate the relations.

XXXI.

As to piety toward the Gods you must know that this is the chief thing, to have right opinions about them, to think that they exist, and that they administer the All well and justly; and you must fix yourself in this principle (duty), to obey them, and yield to them in everything which happens, and voluntarily to follow it as being accomplished by the wisest intelligence. For if you do so, you will never either blame the Gods, nor will you accuse them of neglecting you. And it is not possible for this to be done in any other way than by withdrawing from the things which are not in our power, and by placing the good and the evil only in those things which are in our power. For if you think that any of the things which are not in our power is good or bad, it is absolutely necessary that, when you do not obtain what you wish, and when you fall into those things which you do not wish, you will find fault and hate those who are the cause of them; for every animal is formed by nature to this, to fly from and to turn from the things which appear harmful and the things which are the cause of the harm, but to follow and admire the things which are useful and the causes of the useful. It is impossible then for a person who thinks that he is harmed to be delighted with that which he thinks to be the cause of the harm, as it is also impossible to be pleased with the harm itself. For this reason also a father is reviled by his son, when he gives no part to his son of the things which are considered to be good: and it was this which made Polynices and Eteocles enemies, the opinion that royal power was a good. It is for this reason that the cultivator of the earth reviles the Gods, for this reason the sailor does, and the merchant, and for this reason those who lose their wives and their children. For where the useful (your interest) is, there also piety is.[12] Consequently he who takes care to desire as he ought and to avoid as he ought, at the same time also cares after piety. But to make libations and to sacrifice and to offer first fruits according to the custom of our fathers, purely and not meanly nor carelessly nor scantily nor above our ability, is a thing which belongs to all to do.

XXXII.

When you have recourse to divination, remember that you do not know how it will turn out, but that you are come to inquire from the diviner. But of what kind it is, you know when you come, if indeed you are a philosopher. For if it is any of the things which are not in our power, it is absolutely necessary that it must be neither good nor bad. Do not then bring to the diviner desire or aversion (ἔκκλισιν): if you do, you will approach him with fear. But having determined in your mind that everything which shall turn out (result) is indifferent, and does not concern you, and whatever it may be, for it will be in your power to use it well, and no man will hinder this, come then with confidence to the Gods as your advisers. And then when any advice shall have been given, remember whom you have taken as advisers, and whom you will have neglected, if you do not obey them. And go to divination, as Socrates said that you ought, about those matters in which all the inquiry has reference to the result, and in which means are not given either by reason nor by any other art for knowing the thing which is the subject of the inquiry. Wherefore when we ought to share a friend's danger or that of our country, you must not consult the diviner whether you ought to share it. For even if the diviner shall tell you that the signs of the victims are unlucky, it is plain that this is a token of death or mutilation of part of the body or of exile. But reason prevails that even with these risks we should share the dangers of our friend and of our country. Therefore attend to the greater diviner, the Pythian God, who ejected from the temple him who did not assist his friend when he was being murdered.

XXXIII.

Immediately prescribe some character and some form to yourself, which you shall observe both when you are alone and when you meet with men.

And let silence be the general rule, or let only what is necessary be said, and in few words. And rarely and when the occasion calls we shall say something; but about none of the common subjects, nor about gladiators, nor horse-races, nor about athletes, nor about eating or drinking, which are the usual subjects; and especially not about men, as blaming them or praising them, or comparing them. If then you are able, bring over by your conversation the conversation of your associates to that which is proper; but if you should happen to be confined to the company of strangers, be silent.

Let not your laughter be much, nor on many occasions, nor excessive.

Refuse altogether to take an oath, if it is possible: if it is not, refuse as far as you are able.

Avoid banquets which are given by strangers and by ignorant persons. But if ever there is occasion to join in them, let your attention be carefully fixed, that you slip not into the manners of the vulgar (the uninstructed). For you must know, that if your companion be impure, he also who keeps company with him must become impure, though he should happen to be pure.

21

Take (apply) the things which relate to the body as far as the bare use, as food, drink, clothing, house, and slaves: but exclude everything which is for show or luxury.

As to pleasure with women, abstain as far as you can before marriage: but if you do indulge in it, do it in the way which is conformable to custom. Do not however be disagreeable to those who indulge in these pleasures, or reprove them; and do not often boast that you do not indulge in them yourself.

If a man has reported to you, that a certain person speaks ill of you, do not make any defense (answer) to what has been told you: but reply, The man did not know the rest of my faults, for he would not have mentioned these only.

It is not necessary to go to the theaters often: but if there is ever a proper occasion for going, do not show yourself as being a partisan of any man except yourself, that is, desire only that to be done which is done, and for him only to gain the prize who gains the prize; for in this way you will meet with no hindrance. But abstain entirely from shouts and laughter at any (thing or person), or violent emotions. And when you are come away, do not talk much about what has passed on the stage, except about that which may lead to your own improvement. For it is plain, if you do talk much that you admired the spectacle (more than you ought).[13]

Do not go to the hearing of certain persons' recitations nor visit them readily.[14] But if you do attend, observe gravity and sedateness, and also avoid making yourself disagreeable.

When you are going to meet with any person, and particularly one of those who are considered to be in a superior condition, place before yourself what Socrates or Zeno would have done in such circumstances, and you will have no difficulty in making a proper use of the occasion.

When you are going to any of those who are in great power, place before yourself that you will not find the man at home, that you will be excluded, that the door will not be opened to you, that the man will not care about you. And if with all this it is your duty to visit him, bear what happens, and never say to yourself that it was not worth the trouble. For this is silly, and marks the character of a man who is offended by externals.

In company take care not to speak much and excessively about your own acts or dangers: for as it is pleasant to you to make mention of your dangers, it is not so pleasant to others to hear what has happened to you. Take care also not to provoke laughter; for this is a slippery way toward vulgar habits, and is also adapted to diminish the respect of your neighbors. It is a dangerous habit also to approach obscene talk. When then anything of this kind happens, if there is a good opportunity, rebuke the man who has proceeded to this talk: but if there is not an opportunity, by your silence at least, and blushing and expression of dissatisfaction by your countenance, show plainly that you are displeased at such talk.

XXXIV.

If you have received the impression of any pleasure, guard yourself against being carried away by it; but let the thing wait for you, and allow yourself a certain delay on your own part. Then think of both times, of the time when you will enjoy the pleasure, and of the time after the enjoyment of the pleasure when you will repent and will reproach yourself. And set against these things how you will rejoice if you have abstained from the pleasure, and how you will commend yourself. But if it seem to you seasonable to undertake (do) the thing, take care that the charm of it, and the pleasure, and the attraction of it shall not conquer you: but set on the other side the consideration how much better it is to be conscious that you have gained this victory.

XXXV.

When you have decided that a thing ought to be done and are doing it, never avoid being seen doing it, though the many shall form an unfavorable opinion about it. For if it is not right to do it, avoid doing the thing; but if it is right, why are you afraid of those who shall find fault wrongly?

XXXVI.

As the proposition it is either day or it is night is of great importance for the disjunctive argument, but for the conjunctive is of no value, so in a symposium (entertainment) to select the larger share is of great value for the body, but for the maintenance of the social feeling is worth nothing. When then you are eating with another, remember to look not only to the value for the body of the things set before you, but also to the value of the behavior toward the host which ought to be observed.

XXXVII.

If you have assumed a character above your strength, you have both acted in this matter in an unbecoming way, and you have neglected that which you might have fulfilled.

XXXVIII.

In walking about as you take care not to step on a nail or to sprain your foot, so take care not to damage your own ruling faculty: and if we observe this rule in every act, we shall undertake the act with more security.

XXXIX.

The measure of possession (property) is to every man the body, as the foot is of the shoe. If then you stand on this rule (the demands of the body), you will maintain the measure: but if you pass beyond it, you must then of necessity be hurried as it were down a precipice. As also in the matter of the shoe, if you go beyond the (necessities of the) foot, the shoe is gilded, then of a purple color, then embroidered: for there is no limit to that which has once passed the true measure.

XL.

Women forthwith from the age of fourteen[15] are called by the men mistresses (dominæ). Therefore since they see that there is nothing else that they can obtain, but only the power of lying with men, they begin to decorate themselves, and to place all their hopes in this. It is worth our while then to take care that they may know that they are valued (by men) for nothing else than appearing (being) decent and modest and discreet.

XLI.

It is a mark of a mean capacity to spend much time on the things which concern the body, such as much exercise, much eating, much drinking, much easing of the body, much copulation. But these things should be done as subordinate things: and let all your care be directed to the mind.

XLII.

When any person treats you ill or speaks ill of you, remember that he does this or says this because he thinks that it is his duty. It is not possible then for him to follow that which seems right to you, but that which seems right to himself. Accordingly if he is wrong in his opinion, he is the person who is hurt, for he is the person who has been deceived; for if a man shall suppose the true conjunction to be false, it is not the conjunction which is hindered, but the man who has been deceived about it. If you proceed then from these opinions, you will be mild in temper to him who reviles you: for say on each occasion, It seemed so to him.

XLIII.

Everything has two handles, the one by which it may be borne, the other by which it may not. If your brother acts unjustly, do not lay hold of the act by that handle wherein he acts unjustly, for this is the handle which cannot be borne; but lay hold of the other, that he is your brother, that he was nurtured with you, and you will lay hold of the thing by that handle by which it can be borne.

XLIV.

These reasonings do not cohere: I am richer than you, therefore I am better than you; I am more eloquent than you, therefore I am better than you. On the contrary these rather cohere, I am richer than you, therefore my possessions are greater than yours: I am more eloquent than you, therefore my speech is superior to yours. But you are neither possession nor speech.

XLV.

Does a man bathe quickly (early)? do not say that he bathes badly, but that he bathes quickly. Does a man drink much wine? do not say that he does this badly, but say that he drinks much. For before you shall have determined the opinion,[16] how do you know whether he is acting wrong? Thus it will not happen to you to comprehend some appearances which are capable of being comprehended, but to assent to others.

XLVI.

On no occasion call yourself a philosopher, and do not speak much among the uninstructed about theorems (philosophical rules, precepts): but do that which follows from them. For example at a banquet do not say how a man ought to eat, but eat as you ought to eat. For remember that in this way Socrates also altogether avoided ostentation: persons used to come to him and ask to be recommended by him to philosophers, and he used to take them to philosophers: so easily did he submit to being overlooked. Accordingly if any conversation should arise among uninstructed persons about any theorem, generally be silent; for there is great danger that you will immediately vomit up what you have not digested. And when a man shall say to you, that you know nothing, and you are not vexed, then be sure that you have begun the work (of philosophy). For even sheep do not vomit up their grass and show to the shepherds how much they have eaten; but when they have internally digested the pasture, they produce externally wool and milk. Do you also show not your theorems to the uninstructed, but show the acts which come from their digestion.

XLVII.

When at a small cost you are supplied with everything for the body, do not be proud of this; nor, if you drink water, say on every occasion, I drink water. But consider first how much more frugal the poor are than we, and how much more enduring of labor. And if you ever wish to exercise yourself in labor and endurance, do it for yourself, and not for others: do not embrace statues. But if you are ever very thirsty, take a draught of cold water, and spit it out, and tell no man.

XLVIII.

The condition and characteristic of an uninstructed person is this: he never expects from himself profit (advantage) nor harm, but from externals. The condition and characteristic of a philosopher is this: he expects all advantage and all harm from himself. The signs (marks) of one who is making progress are these: he censures no man, he praises no man, he blames no man, he accuses no man, he says nothing about himself as if he were somebody or knew something; when he is impeded at all or hindered, he blames himself: if a man praises him, he ridicules the praiser to himself: if a man censures him, he makes no defense: he goes about like weak persons, being careful not to move any of the things which are placed, before they are firmly fixed: he removes all desire from himself, and he transfers aversion (ἔκκλιοιυ) to those things only of the things within our power which are contrary to nature: he employs a moderate movement toward everything: whether he is considered foolish or ignorant, he cares not: and in a word he watches himself as if he were an enemy and lying in ambush.

XLIX.

When a man is proud because he can understand and explain the writings of Chrysippus, say to yourself, if Chrysippus had not written obscurely, this man would have had nothing to be proud of. But what is it that I wish? To understand Nature and to follow it. I inquire therefore who is the interpreter: and when I have heard that it is Chrysippus, I come to him (the interpreter). But I do not understand what is written, and therefore I seek the interpreter. And so far there is yet nothing to be proud of. But when I shall have found the interpreter, the thing that remains is to use the precepts (the lessons). This itself is the only thing to be proud of. But if I shall admire the exposition, what else have I been made unless a grammarian instead of a philosopher? except in one thing, that I am explaining Chrysippus instead of Homer. When then any man says to me, Read Chrysippus to me, I rather blush, when I cannot show my acts like to and consistent with his words.

L.

Whatever things (rules) are proposed[17] to you [for the conduct of life] abide by them, as if they were laws, as if you would be guilty of impiety if you transgressed any of them. And whatever any man shall say about you, do not attend to it: for this is no affair of yours. How long will you then still defer thinking yourself worthy of the best things, and in no matter transgressing the distinctive reason? Have you accepted the theorems (rules), which it was your duty to agree to, and have you agreed to them? what teacher then do you still expect that you defer to him the correction of yourself? You are no longer a youth, but already a full-grown man. If then you are negligent and slothful, and are continually making procrastination after procrastination, and proposal (intention) after proposal, and fixing day after day, after which you will attend to yourself, you will not know that you are not making improvement, but you will continue ignorant (uninstructed) both while you live and till you die. Immediately then think it right to live as a full-grown man, and one who is making proficiency, and let everything which appears to you to be the best be to you a law which must not be transgressed. And if anything laborious, or pleasant or glorious or inglorious be presented to you, remember that now is the contest, now are the Olympic games, and they cannot be deferred; and that it depends on one defeat and one giving way that progress is either lost or maintained. Socrates in this way became perfect, in all things improving himself, attending to nothing except to reason. But you, though you are not yet a Socrates, ought to live as one who wishes to be a Socrates.

LI.

The first and most necessary place (part) in philosophy is the use of theorems (precepts), for instance, that we must not lie: the second part is that of demonstrations, for instance, How is it proved that we ought not to lie: the third is that which is confirmatory of these two and explanatory, for example, How is this a demonstration? For what is demonstration, what is consequence, what is contradiction, what is truth, what is falsehood? The third part (topic) is necessary on account of the second, and the second on account of the first; but the most necessary and that on which we ought to rest is the first. But we do the contrary. For we spend our time on the third topic, and all our earnestness is about it: but we entirely neglect the first. Therefore we lie; but the demonstration that we ought not to lie we have ready to hand.

LII.

In every thing (circumstance) we should hold these maxims ready to hand:

> Lead me, O Zeus, and thou O Destiny,
> The way that I am bid by you to go:
> To follow I am ready. If I choose not,
> I make myself a wretch, and still must follow.[18]

> But whoso nobly yields unto necessity,
> We hold him wise, and skill'd in things divine.[19]

And the third also: O Crito, if so it pleases the Gods, so let it be; Anytus and Melitus are able indeed to kill me, but they cannot harm me.[20]

FRAGMENTS
OF
EPICTETUS

These Fragments are entitled "Epicteti Fragmenta maxime ex Ioanne Stobæo, Antonio, et Maximo collecta" (ed. Schweig.). There are some notes and emendations on the Fragments; and a short dissertation on them by Schweighaeuser.

Nothing is known of Stobæus nor of his time, except the fact that he has preserved some extracts of an ethical kind from the New Platonist Hierocles, who lived about the middle of the fifth century CE; and it is therefore concluded that Stobæus lived after Hierocles. The fragments attributed to Epictetus are preserved by Stobæus in his work entitled Ἀνθολόγιον, or Florilegium or Sermones.

Antonius Monachus, a Greek monk, also made a Florilegium, entitled Melissa (the bee). His date is uncertain, but it was certainly much later than the time of Stobæus.

Maximus, also named the monk, and reverenced as a saint, is said to have been a native of Constantinople, and born about 580 CE.

Some of the Fragments contained in the edition of Schweighaeuser are certainly not from Epictetus. Many of the fragments are obscure; but they are translated as accurately as I can translate them, and the reader must give to them such meaning as he can.

I.

The life which is implicated with fortune (depends on fortune) is like a winter torrent: for it is turbulent, and full of mud, and difficult to cross, and tyrannical, and noisy, and of short duration.

II.

A soul which is conversant with virtue is like an ever-flowing source, for it is pure and tranquil and potable and sweet and communicative (social), and rich and harmless and free from mischief.

III.

If you wish to be good, first believe that you are bad.

IV.

It is better to do wrong seldom and to own it, and to act right for the most part, than seldom to admit that you have done wrong and to do wrong often.

V.

Check (punish) your passions that you may not be punished by them.

VI.

Do not so much be ashamed of that (disgrace) which proceeds from men's opinions as fly from that which comes from the truth.

VII.

If you wish to be well spoken of, learn to speak well (of others): and when you have learned to speak well of them, try to act well, and so you will reap the fruit of being well spoken of.

VIII.

Freedom and slavery, the one is the name of virtue, and the other of vice: and both are acts of the will. But where there is no will, neither of them touches (affects) these things. But the soul is accustomed to be master of the body, and the things which belong to the body have no share in the will. For no man is a slave who is free in his will.

IX.

It is an evil chain, fortune (a chain) of the body, and vice of the soul. For he who is loose (free) in the body, but bound in the soul is a slave: but on the contrary he who is bound in the body, but free (unbound) in the soul, is free.

X.

The bond of the body is loosened by nature through death, and by vice through money:[21] but the bond of the soul is loosened by learning, and by experience and by discipline.

XI.

If you wish to live without perturbation and with pleasure, try to have all who dwell with you good. And you will have them good, if you instruct the willing, and dismiss those who are unwilling (to be taught): for there will fly away together with those who have fled away both wickedness and slavery; and there will be left with those who remain with you goodness and liberty.

XII.

It is a shame for those who sweeten drink with the gifts of the bees, by badness to embitter reason which is the gift of the gods.

XIII.

No man who loves money, and loves pleasure, and loves fame, also loves mankind, but only he who loves virtue.

XIV.

As you would not choose to sail in a large and decorated and gold-laden ship (or ship ornamented with gold), and to be drowned; so do not choose to dwell in a large and costly house and to be disturbed (by cares).

XV.

When we have been invited to a banquet, we take what is set before us: but if a guest should ask the host to set before him fish or sweet cakes, he would be considered to be an unreasonable fellow. But in the world we ask the Gods for what they do not give; and we do this though the things are many which they have given.

XVI.

They are amusing fellows, said he (Epictetus), who are proud of the things which are not in our power. A man says, I am better than you, for I possess much land, and you are wasting with hunger. Another says, I am of consular rank. Another says, I am a Procurator (ἐπίτροπος). Another, I have curly hair. But a horse does not say to a horse, I am superior to you, for I possess much fodder, and much barley, and my bits are of gold and my harness is embroidered: but he says, I am swifter than you. And every animal is better or worse from his own merit (virtue) or his own badness. Is there then no virtue in man only? and must we look to the hair, and our clothes and to our ancestors?

XVII.

The sick are vexed with the physician who gives them no advice, and think that he has despaired of them. But why should they not have the same feeling toward the philosopher, and think that he has despaired of their coming to a sound state of mind, if he says nothing at all that is useful to a man?

XVIII.

Those who are well constituted in the body endure both heat and cold: and so those who are well constituted in the soul endure both anger and grief and excessive joy and the other affects.

XIX.

Examine yourself whether you wish to be rich or to be happy. If you wish to be rich, you should know that it is neither a good thing nor at all in your power: but if you wish to be happy, you should know that it is both a good thing and in your power, for the one is a temporary loan of fortune, and happiness comes from the will.

XX.

As when you see a viper or an asp or a scorpion in an ivory or golden box, you do not on account of the costliness of the material love it or think it happy, but because the nature of it is pernicious, you turn away from it and loath it; so when you shall see vice dwelling in wealth and in the swollen fullness of fortune, be not struck by the splendor of the material, but despise the false character of the morals.

XXI.

Wealth is not one of the good things; great expenditure is one of the bad; moderation is one of the good things. And moderation invites to frugality and the acquisition of good things: but wealth invites to great expenditure and draws us away from moderation. It is difficult then for a rich man to be moderate, or for a moderate man to be rich.[22]

XXII.

As if you were begotten or born in a ship, you would not be eager to be the master of it, so—[23] For neither there (in the ship) will the ship naturally be connected with you, nor wealth in the other case; but reason is everywhere naturally connected with you. As then reason is a thing which naturally belongs to you and is born in you, consider this also as specially your own and take care of it.

XXIII.

If you had been born among the Persians, you would not have wished to live in Hellas (Greece), but to have lived in Persia happy: so if you are born in poverty, why do you seek to grow rich, and why do you not remain in poverty and be happy?[24]

XXIV.

As it is better to lie compressed in a narrow bed and be healthy than to be tossed with disease on a broad couch, so also it is better to contract yourself within a small competence and to be happy than to have a great fortune and to be wretched.

XXV.

It is not poverty which produces sorrow, but desire; nor does wealth release from fear, but reason (the power of reasoning). If then you acquire this power of reasoning, you will neither desire wealth nor complain of poverty.

XXVI.

Neither is a horse elated nor proud of his manger and trappings and coverings, nor a bird of his little shreds of cloth and of his nest: but both of them are proud of their swiftness, one proud of the swiftness of the feet, and the other of the wings. Do you also then not be greatly proud of your food and dress and, in short, of any external things, but be proud of your integrity and good deeds.

XXVII.

To live well differs from living extravagantly: for the first comes from moderation and a sufficiency and good order and propriety and frugality; but the other comes from intemperance and luxury and want of order and want of propriety. And the end (the consequence) of the one is true praise, but of the other blame. If then you wish to live well, do not seek to be commended for profuse expenditure.

XXVIII.

Let the measure to you of all food and drink be the first satisfying of the desire; and let the food and the pleasure be the desire (appetite) itself: and you will neither take more than is necessary, nor will you want cooks, and you will be satisfied with the drink that comes in the way.

XXIX.

Make your manner of eating neither luxurious nor gloomy, but lively and frugal, that the soul may not be perturbed through being deceived by the pleasures of the body, and that it may despise them; and that the soul may not be injured by the enjoyment of present luxury and the body may not afterward suffer from disease.[25]

XXX.

Take care that the food which you put into the stomach does not fatten (nourish) you, but the cheerfulness of the mind: for the food is changed into excrement, and ejected, and the urine also flows out at the same time; but the cheerfulness, even if the soul be separated, remains always uncorrupted.[26]

XXXI.

In banquets remember that you entertain two guests, body and soul: and whatever you shall have given to the body you soon eject: but what you shall have given to the soul, you keep always.

XXXII.

Do not mix anger with profuse expenditure and serve them up to your guests. Profusion which fills the body is quickly gone; but anger sinks into the soul and remains for a long time. Consider then that you be not transported with anger and insult your guests at a great expense; but rather please them with frugality and by gentle behavior.

XXXIII.

In your banquets (meals) take care that those who serve (your slaves) are not more than those who are served; for it is foolish for many souls (persons) to wait on a few couches (seats).

XXXIV.

It is best if even in the preparations for a feast you take a part of the labor, and at the enjoyment of the food, while you are feasting, you share with those who serve the things which are before you. But if such behavior be unsuitable to the occasion, remember that you are served when you are not laboring by those who are laboring, when you are eating by those who are not eating, when you are drinking by those who are not drinking, while you are talking by those who are silent, while you are at ease by those who are under constraint; and if you remember this, you will neither being heated with anger be guilty of any absurdity yourself, nor by irritating another will you cause any mischief.[27]

XXXV.

Quarreling and contention are everywhere foolish, and particularly in talk over wine they are unbecoming: for a man who is drunk could not teach a man who is sober, nor on the other hand could a drunken man be convinced by a sober man. But where there is no sobriety, it will appear that to no purpose have you labored for the result of persuasion.[28]

XXXVI.

Grasshoppers (cicadæ) are musical: snails have no voice. Snails have pleasure in being moist, but grasshoppers in being dry. Next the dew invites forth the snails, and for this they crawl out: but on the contrary the sun when he is hot, rouses the grasshoppers and they sing in the sun. Therefore if you wish to be a musical man and to harmonize well with others, when over the cups the soul is bedewed with wine, at that time do not permit the soul to go forth and to be polluted; but when in company (parties) it is fired by reason, then bid her to utter oracular words and to sing the oracles of justice.

XXXVII.

Examine in three ways him who is talking with you, as superior, or as inferior, or as equal: and if he is superior, you should listen to him and be convinced by him: but if he is inferior, you should convince him; if he is equal, you should agree with him; and thus you will never be guilty of being quarrelsome.

XXXVIII.

It is better by assenting to truth to conquer opinion, than by assenting to opinion to be conquered by truth.

XXXIX.

If you seek truth, you will not seek by every means to gain a victory; and if you have found truth, you will have the gain of not being defeated.

XL.

Truth conquers with itself; but opinion conquers among those who are external.[29]

XLI.

It is better to live with one free man and to be without fear and free, than to be a slave with many.

XLII.

What you avoid suffering, do not attempt to make others suffer. You avoid slavery: take care that others are not your slaves. For if you endure to have a slave, you appear to be a slave yourself first. For vice has no community with virtue, nor freedom with slavery.

XLIII.

As he who is in health would not choose to be served (ministered to) by the sick, nor for those who dwell with him to be sick, so neither would a free man endure to be served by slaves, or for those who live with him to be slaves.

XLIV.

Whoever you are who wish to be not among the number of slaves, release yourself from slavery: and you will be free, if you are released from desire. For neither Aristides nor Epaminondas nor Lycurgus through being rich and served by slaves were named the one just, the other a god, and the third a savior, but because they were poor and delivered Hellas (Greece) from slavery.[30]

XLV.

If you wish your house to be well managed, imitate the Spartan Lycurgus. For as he did not fence his city with walls, but fortified the inhabitants by virtue and preserved the city always free;[31] so do you not cast around (your house) a large court and raise high towers, but strengthen the dwellers by good-will and fidelity and friendship, and then nothing harmful will enter it, not even if the whole band of wickedness shall array itself against it.

XLVI.

Do not hang your house round with tablets and pictures, but decorate it with moderation: for the one is of a foreign (unsuitable) kind, and a temporary deception of the eyes; but the other is a natural and indelible, and perpetual ornament of the house.

XLVII.

Instead of a herd of oxen, endeavor to assemble herds of friends in your house.

XLVIII.

As a wolf resembles a dog, so both a flatterer, and an adulterer and a parasite, resemble a friend. Take care then that instead of watch-dogs you do not without knowing it let in mischievous wolves.

XLIX.

To be eager that your house should be admired by being whitened with gypsum, is the mark of a man who has no taste: but to set off (decorate) our morals by the goodness of our communication (social habits) is the mark of a man who is a lover of beauty and a lover of man.

L.

If you begin by admiring little things, you will not be thought worthy of great things: but if you despise the little, you will be greatly admired.

LI.

Nothing is smaller (meaner) than love of pleasure, and love of gain and pride. Nothing is superior to magnanimity, and gentleness, and love of mankind, and beneficence.

LII.

They bring forward (they name, they mention) the peevish philosophers (the Stoics), whose opinion it is that pleasure is not a thing conformable to nature, but is a thing which is consequent on the things which are conformable to nature, as justice, temperance, freedom. What then? is the soul pleased and made tranquil by the pleasures of the body which are smaller, as Epicurus says; and is it not pleased with its own good things, which are the greatest? And indeed nature has given to me modesty, and I blush much when I think of saying anything base (indecent). This motion (feeling) does not permit me to make (consider) pleasure the good and the end (purpose) of life.

LIII.

In Rome the women have in their hands Plato's Polity (the Republic), because it allows (advises) the women to be common, for they attend only to the words of Plato, not to his meaning. Now he does not recommend marriage and one man to cohabit with one woman, and then that the women should be common: but he takes away such a marriage, and introduces another kind of marriage. And in fine, men are pleased with finding excuses for their faults. Yet philosophy says that we ought not to stretch out even a finger without a reason.

LIV.

Of pleasures those which occur most rarely give the greatest delight.

LV.

If a man should transgress moderation, the things which give the greatest delight would become the things which give the least.

LVI.

It is just to commend Agrippinus for this reason, that though he was a man of the highest worth, he never praised himself; but even if another person praised him, he would blush. And he was such a man (Epictetus said) that he would write in praise of anything disagreeable that befell him; if it was a fever, he would write of a fever; if he was disgraced, he would write of disgrace; if he were banished, of banishment. And on one occasion (he mentioned) when he was going to dine, a messenger brought him news that Nero commanded him to go into banishment; on which Agrippinus said, Well then we will dine at Aricia.

LVII.

Diogenes said that no labor was good, unless the end (purpose) of it was courage and strength of the soul, but not of the body.

LVIII.

As a true balance is neither corrected by a true balance nor judged by a false balance, so also a just judge is neither corrected by just judges nor is he judged (condemned) by unjust judges.

LIX.

As that which is straight does not need that which is straight, so neither does the just need that which is just.

LX.

Do not give judgment in one court (of justice) before you have been tried yourself before justice.[32]

LXI.

If you wish to make your judgments just, listen not to (regard not) any of those who are parties (to the suit), nor to those who plead in it, but listen to justice itself.

LXII.

You will fail (stumble) least in your judgments, if you yourself fail (stumble) least in your life.

LXIII.

It is better when you judge justly to be blamed undeservedly by him who has been condemned than when you judge unjustly to be justly blamed by (before) nature.

LXIV.

As the stone which tests the gold is not at all tested itself by the gold, so it is with him who has the faculty of judging.

LXV.

It is shameful for the judge to be judged by others.

LXVI.

As nothing is straighter than that which is straight, so nothing is juster than that which is just.

LXVII.

Who among us does not admire the act of Lycurgus the Lacedæmonian? For after he was maimed in one of his eyes by one of the citizens, and the young man was delivered up to him by the people that he might punish him as he chose, Lycurgus spared him: and after instructing him and making him a good man he brought him into the theater. When the Lacedæmonians expressed their surprise, Lycurgus said, I received from you this youth when he was insolent and violent: I restore him to you gentle and a good citizen.

LXVIII.

Pittacus after being wronged by a certain person and having the power of punishing him let him go, saying, Forgiveness is better than revenge: for forgiveness is the sign of a gentle nature, but revenge the sign of a savage nature.[33]

LXIX.

But before everything this is the act of nature to bind together and to fit together the movement toward the appearance of that which is becoming (fit) and useful.

LXX.

To suppose that we shall be easily despised by others, if we do not in every way do some damage to those who first show us their hostility, is the mark of very ignoble and foolish men: for (thus) we affirm that the man is considered to be contemptible because of his inability to do what is good (useful).

LXXI.

When you are attacking (or going to attack) any person violently and with threats, remember to say to yourself first, that you are (by nature) mild (gentle); and if you do nothing savage, you will continue to live without repentance and without blame.

LXXII.

A man ought to know that it is not easy for him to have an opinion (or fixed principle), if he does not daily say the same things, and hear the same things, and at the same time apply them to life.

LXXIII.

[Nicias was so fond of labor (assiduous) that he often asked his slaves, if he had bathed and if he had dined.]

LXXIV.

[The slaves of Archimedes used to drag him by force from his table of diagrams and anoint him; and Archimedes would then draw his figures on his own body when it had been anointed.]

LXXV.

[Lampis the shipowner being asked how he acquired his wealth, answered, With no difficulty, my great wealth; but my small wealth (my first gains), with much labor.]

LXXVI.

Solon having been asked by Periander over their cups (παρά πότον), since he happened to say nothing, Whether he was silent for want of words or because he was a fool, replied: No fool is able to be silent over his cups.

LXXVII.

Attempt on every occasion to provide for nothing so much as that which is safe: for silence is safer than speaking. And omit speaking whatever is without sense and reason.

LXXVIII.

As the fire-lights in harbors by a few pieces of dry wood raises a great flame and give sufficient help to ships which are wandering on the sea; so also an illustrious man in a state which is tempest-tossed, while he is himself satisfied with a few things does great services to his citizens.

LXXIX.

As if you attempted to manage a ship, you would certainly learn completely the steersman's art, [so if you would administer a state, learn the art of managing a state]. For it will be in your power, as in the first case to manage the whole ship, so in the second case also to manage the whole state.

LXXX.

If you propose to adorn your city by the dedication of offerings (monuments), first dedicate to yourself (decorate yourself with) the noblest offering of gentleness, and justice and beneficence.

LXXXI.

You will do the greatest services to the state, if you shall raise not the roofs of the houses, but the souls of the citizens: for it is better that great souls should dwell in small houses than for mean slaves to lurk in great houses.

LXXXII.

Do not decorate the walls of your house with the valuable stones from Eubœa and Sparta; but adorn the minds (breasts) of the citizens and of those who administer the state with the instruction which comes from Hellas (Greece). For states are well governed by the wisdom (judgment) of men, but not by stone and wood.[34]

LXXXIII.

As, if you wished to breed lions, you would not care about the costliness of their dens, but about the habits of the animals; so, if you attempt to preside over your citizens, be not so anxious about the costliness of the buildings as careful about the manly character of those who dwell in them.

LXXXIV.[35]

As a skillful horse-trainer does not feed (only) the good colts and allow to starve those who are disobedient to the rein, but he feeds both alike, and chastises the one more and forces him to be equal to the other: so also a careful man and one who is skilled in political power, attempts to treat well those citizens who have a good character, but does not will that those who are of a contrary character should be ruined at once; and he in no manner grudges both of them their food, but he teaches and urges on with more vehemence him who resists reason and law.

LXXXV.

As a goose is not frightened by cackling nor a sheep by bleating, so let not the clamor of a senseless multitude alarm you.

LXXXVI.

As a multitude, when they without reason demand of you anything of your own, do not disconcert you, so do not be moved from your purpose even by a rabble when they unjustly attempt to move you.

LXXXVII.

What is due to the state pay as quickly as you can, and you will never be asked for that which is not due.

LXXXVIII.

As the sun does not wait for prayers and incantations to be induced to rise, but immediately shines and is saluted by all: so do you also not wait for clappings of hands, and shouts and praise to be induced to do good, but be a doer of good voluntarily, and you will be beloved as much as the sun.

LXXXIX.

Neither should a ship rely on one small anchor, nor should life rest on a single hope.

XC.

We ought to stretch our legs and stretch our hopes only to that which is possible.

XCI.

When Thales was asked what is most universal, he answered, Hope, for hope stays with those who have nothing else.

XCII.

It is more necessary to heal the soul than the body, for to die is better than to live a bad life.

XCIII.

Pyrrho used to say that there is no difference between dying and living: and a man said to him, Why then do you not die? Pyrrho replied, Because there is no difference.

XCIV.[36]

Admirable is nature, and, as Xenophon says, a lover of animated beings. The body then, which is of all things the most unpleasant and the most foul (dirty), we love and take care of; for if we were obliged for five days only to take care of our neighbor's body, we should not be able to endure it. Consider then what a thing it would be to rise in the morning and rub the teeth of another, and after doing some of the necessary offices to wash those parts. In truth it is wonderful that we love a thing to which we perform such services every day. I fill this bag, and then I empty it;[37] what is more troublesome? But I must act as the servant of God. For this reason I remain (here), and I endure to wash this miserable body, to feed it and to clothe it. But when I was younger, God imposed on me also another thing, and I submitted to it. Why then do you not submit, when Nature who has given us this body takes it away? I love the body, you may say. Well, as I said just now, Nature gave you also this love of the body: but Nature says, Leave it now, and have no more trouble (with it).

XCV.

When a man dies young, he blames the gods. When he is old and does not die, he blames the gods because he suffers when he ought to have already ceased from suffering. And nevertheless, when death approaches, he wishes to live, and sends to the physician and entreats him to omit no care or trouble. Wonderful, he said, are men, who are neither willing to live nor to die.

XCVI.

To the longer life and the worse, the shorter life, if it is better, ought by all means to be preferred.

XCVII.

When we are children our parents deliver us to a pedagogue to take care on all occasions that we suffer no harm. But when we are become men, God delivers us to our innate conscience to take care of us. This guardianship then we must in no way despise, for we shall both displease God and be enemies to our own conscience.

XCVIII.

[We ought to use wealth as the material for some act, not for every act alike.]

XCIX.

[Virtue then should be desired by all men more than wealth which is dangerous to the foolish; for the wickedness of men is increased by wealth. And the more a man is without sense, the more violent is he in excess, for he has the means of satisfying his mad desire for pleasures.]

C.

What we ought not to do, we should not even think of doing.

CI.

Deliberate much before saying or doing anything, for you will not have the power of recalling what has been said or done.

CII.

Every place is safe to him who lives with justice.

CIII.

Crows devour the eyes of the dead, when the dead have no longer need of them. But flatterers destroy the souls of the living and blind their eyes.

CIV.

The anger of an ape and the threats of a flatterer should be considered as the same.

CV.

Listen to those who wish to advise what is useful, but not to those who are eager to flatter on all occasions; for the first really see what is useful, but the second look to that which agrees with the opinion of those who possess power, and imitating the shadows of bodies they assent to what is said by the powerful.

CVI.

The man who gives advice ought first to have regard to the modesty and character (reputation) of those whom he advises; for those who have lost the capacity of blushing are incorrigible.

CVII.

To admonish is better than to reproach: for admonition is mild and friendly, but reproach is harsh and insulting; and admonition corrects those who are doing wrong, but reproach only convicts them.

CVIII.

Give of what you have to strangers and to those who have need: for he who gives not to him who wants, will not receive himself when he wants.

CIX.

A pirate had been cast on the land and was perishing through the tempest. A man took clothing and gave it to him, and brought the pirate into his house, and supplied him with everything else that was necessary. When the man was reproached by a person for doing kindness to the bad, he replied, I have shown this regard not to the man, but to mankind.[38]

CX.

A man should choose (pursue) not every pleasure, but the pleasure which leads to goodness.

CXI.

It is the part of a wise man to resist pleasures, but of a foolish man to be a slave to them.

CXII.

Pleasure, like a kind of bait, is thrown before (in front of) everything which is really bad, and easily allures greedy souls to the hook of perdition.

CXIII.

Choose rather to punish your appetites than to be punished through them.

CXIV.

No man is free who is not master of himself.

CXV.

The vine bears three bunches of grapes: the first is that of pleasure, the second of drunkenness, the third of violence.

CXVI.

Over your wine do not talk much to display your learning; for you will utter bilious stuff.

CXVII.

He is intoxicated who drinks more than three cups: and if he is not intoxicated, he has exceeded moderation.

CXVIII.

Let your talk of God be renewed every day, rather than your food.

CXIX.

Think of God more frequently than you breathe.

CXX.

If you always remember that whatever you are doing in the soul or in the body, God stands by as an inspector, you will never err (do wrong) in all your prayers and in all your acts, but you will have God dwelling with you.[39]

CXXI.

As it is pleasant to see the sea from the land, so it is pleasant for him who has escaped from troubles to think of them.

CXXII.

Law intends indeed to do service to human life, but it is not able when men do not choose to accept her services; for it is only in those who are obedient to her that she displays her special virtue.

CXXIII.

As to the sick physicians are as saviors, so to those also who are wronged are the laws.

CXXIV.

The justest laws are those which are the truest.

CXXV.

To yield to law and to a magistrate and to him who is wiser than yourself, is becoming.

CXXVI.

The things which are done contrary to law are the same as things which are not done.

CXXVII.

In prosperity it is very easy to find a friend; but in adversity it is most difficult of all things.

CXXVIII.

Time relieves the foolish from sorrow, but reason relieves the wise.

CXXIX.

He is a wise man who does not grieve for the things which he has not, but rejoices for those which he has.

CXXX.

Epictetus being asked how a man should give pain to his enemy answered, By preparing himself to live the best life that he can.

CXXXI.

Let no wise man be averse to undertaking the office of a magistrate: for it is both impious for a man to withdraw himself from being useful to those who have need of our services, and it is ignoble to give way to the worthless; for it is foolish to prefer being ill-governed to governing well.

CXXXII.

Nothing is more becoming to him who governs than to despise no man and not show arrogance, but to preside over all with equal care.

CXXXIII.

[In poverty any man lives (can live) happily, but very seldom in wealth and power. The value of poverty excels so much that no just man would exchange poverty for disreputable wealth, unless indeed the richest of the Athenians Themistocles, the son of Neocles, was better than Aristides and Socrates, though he was poor in virtue. But the wealth of Themistocles and Themistocles himself have perished and have left no name. For all things die with death in a bad man, but the good is eternal.]⁴⁰

CXXXIV.

Remember that such was, and is, and will be the nature of the universe, and that it is not possible that the things which come into being can come into being otherwise than they do now; and that not only men have participated in this change and transmutation, and all other living things which are on the earth, but also the things which are divine. And indeed the very four elements are changed and transmuted up and down, and earth becomes water and water becomes air, and the air again is transmuted into other things, and the same manner of transmutation takes place from above to below. If a man attempts to turn his mind toward these thoughts, and to persuade himself to accept with willingness that which is necessary, he will pass through life with complete moderation and harmony.

CXXXV.

He who is dissatisfied with things present and what is given by fortune is an ignorant man in life: but he who bears them nobly and rationally and the things which proceed from them is worthy of being considered a good man.

CXXXVI.

All things obey and serve the world (the universe), earth and sea and sun and the rest of the stars, and the plants of earth and animals. And our body obeys it also both in disease and in health when it (the universe) chooses, both in youth and in age, and when it is passing through the other changes. What is reasonable then and in our power is this, for our judgment not to be the only thing which resists it (the universe): for it is strong and superior, and it has determined better about us by administering (governing) us also together with the whole. And besides, this opposition also is unreasonable and does nothing more than cause us to be tormented uselessly and to fall into pain and sorrow.

The fragments which follow are in part assigned to Epictetus, in part to others.

CXXXVII.

Contentment, as it is a short road and pleasant, has great delight and little trouble.

CXXXVIII.

Fortify yourself with contentment, for this is an impregnable fortress.

CXXXIX.

Let nothing be valued more than truth: not even selection of a friendship which lies without the influence of the affects, by which (affects) justice is both confounded (disturbed) and darkened.[41]

CXL.

Truth is a thing immortal and perpetual, and it gives to us a beauty which fades not away in time nor does it take away the freedom of speech which proceeds from justice; but it gives to us the knowledge of what is just and lawful, separating from them the unjust and refuting them.

CXLI.

We should not have either a blunt knife or a freedom of speech which is ill-managed.

CXLII.

Nature has given to men one tongue, but two ears, that we may hear from others twice as much as we speak.

CXLIII.

Nothing really pleasant or unpleasant subsists by nature, but all things become so through habit (custom).

CXLIV.

Choose the best life, for custom (habit) will make it pleasant.

CXLV.

Be careful to leave your sons well instructed rather than rich, for the hopes of the instructed are better than the wealth of the ignorant.

CXLVI.

A daughter is a possession to her father which is not his own.

CXLVII.

The same person advised to leave modesty to children rather than gold.

CXLVIII.

The reproach of a father is agreeable medicine, for it contains more that is useful than it contains of that which gives pain.

CXLIX.

He who has been lucky in a son-in-law has found a son: but he who has been unlucky, has lost also a daughter.

CL.

The value of education (knowledge) like that of gold is valued in every place.

CLI.

He who exercises wisdom exercises the knowledge which is about God.

CLII.

Nothing among animals is so beautiful as a man adorned by learning (knowledge).

CLIII.

We ought to avoid the friendship of the bad and the enmity of the good.

CLIV.

The necessity of circumstances proves friends and detects enemies.

CLV.

When our friends are present, we ought to treat them well; and when they are absent, to speak of them well.

CLVI.

Let no man think that he is loved by any man when he loves no man.

CLVII.

You ought to choose both physician and friend not the most agreeable, but the most useful.

CLVIII.

If you wish to live a life free from sorrow, think of what is going to happen as if it had already happened.

CLIX.

Be free from grief not through insensibility like the irrational animals, nor through want of thought like the foolish, but like a man of virtue by having reason as the consolation of grief.

CLX.

Whoever are least disposed in mind by calamities, and in act struggle most against them, these are the best men in states and in private life.

CLXI.

Those who have been instructed, like those who have been trained in the palæstra, though they may have fallen, rise again from their misfortune quickly and skillfully.

CLXII.

We ought to call in reason like a good physician as a help in misfortune.

CLXIII.

A fool having enjoyed good fortune like intoxication to a great amount becomes more foolish.

CLXIV.

Envy is the antagonist of the fortunate.

CLXV.

He who bears in mind what man is will never be troubled at anything which happens.

CLXVI.

For making a good voyage a pilot (master) and wind are necessary: and for happiness, reason and art.

CLXVII.

We should enjoy good fortune while we have it, like the fruits of autumn.

CLXVIII.

He is unreasonable who is grieved (troubled) at the things which happen from the necessity of nature.

Some Fragments of Epictetus Omitted
by Upton and by Meibomius.

CLXIX.

Of the things which are, God has put some of them in our power, and some he has not. In our own power he has placed that which is the best and the most important, that indeed through which he himself is happy, the use of appearances. For when the use is rightly employed, there is freedom, happiness, tranquillity, constancy: and this is also justice and law, and temperance, and every virtue. But all other things he has not placed in our power. Wherefore we also ought to be of one mind with God, and making this division of things, to look after those which are in our power; and of the things not in our power, to intrust them to the Universe, and whether it should require our children, or our country, or our body, or anything else, willingly to give them up.[42]

CLXX.

When a young man was boasting in the theater and saying, I am wise, for I have conversed with many wise men; Epictetus said, I also have conversed with many rich men, but I am not rich.

CLXXI.

The same person said, It is not good for him who has been well taught to talk among the untaught, as it is not right for him who is sober to talk among those who are drunk.

CLXXII.

Epictetus being asked, What man is rich, answered, He who is content (who has enough).

CLXXIII.

Xanthippe was blaming Socrates, because he was making small preparation for receiving his friends: but Socrates said, If they are our friends, they will not care about it; and if they are not, we shall care nothing about them.

CLXXIV.

When Archelaus was sending for Socrates to make him rich, Socrates told the messengers to return this answer: At Athens four measures (chœnices) of meal are sold for one obolus (the sixth of a drachma), and the fountains run with water: if what I have is not enough (sufficient) for me, yet I am sufficient for what I have, and so it becomes sufficient for me. Do you not see that it was with no nobler voice that Polus acted the part of Œdipus as king than of Œdipus as a wanderer and beggar at Colonus? Then shall the good man appear to be inferior to Polus, and unable to act well every character (personage) imposed on him by the Deity? and shall he not imitate Ulysses, who even in rags made no worse figure than in the soft purple robe?

CLXXV.

What do I care, he (Epictetus) says, whether all things are composed of atoms, or of similar parts or of fire and earth? for is it not enough to know the nature of the good and the evil, and the measures of the desires and the aversions, and also the movements toward things and from them; and using these as rules to administer the affairs of life, but not to trouble ourselves about the things above us? For these things are perhaps incomprehensible to the human mind: and if any man should even suppose them to be in the highest degree comprehensible, what then is the profit of them, if they are comprehended? And must we not say that those men have needless trouble who assign these things as necessary to the philosopher's discourse? Is then also the precept written at Delphi superfluous, which is Know thyself? It is not so, he says. What then is the meaning of it? If a man gave to a choreutes (member of chorus) the precept to know himself, would he not have observed in the precept that he must direct his attention to himself?

CLXXVI.

You are a little soul carrying a dead body, as Epictetus said.

CLXXVII.

He (Epictetus) said that he had discovered an art in giving assent; and in the topic (matter) of the movements he had discovered that we must observe attention, that the movements be subject to exception, that they be social, that they be according to the worth of each thing; and that we ought to abstain entirely from desire, and to employ aversion to none of the things which are not in our power.

CLXXVIII.

About no common thing, he said, the contest (dispute) is, but about being mad or not.

Endnotes

1. Appearances are named "harsh" or "rough" when they are "contrary to reason and overexciting and in fact make life rough (uneven) by the want of symmetry and by inequality in the movements." Simplicius, v. (i. 5).
2. Upton proposes to read "elated at something good which is in the horse." I think that he is right.
3. He means, Do not chastise your slave while you are in a passion, lest, while you are trying to correct him, and it is very doubtful whether you will succeed, you fall into a vice which is a man's great and only calamity. Schweig.
4. The passage seems to mean, that your slave has not the power of disturbing you, because you have the power of not being disturbed. See Upton's note on the text.
5. When Epictetus says "you would have badness not to be badness," he means that "badness" is in the will of him who has the badness, and as you wish to subject it to your will, you are a fool. It is your business, as far as you can, to improve the slave: you may wish this. It is his business to obey your instruction: this is what he ought to wish to do; but for him to will to do this, that lies in himself, not in you. Schweig.

6. This is obscure. "It is true that the man is wretched, not because of the things external which have happened to him, but through the fact that he allows himself to be affected so much by external things which are placed out of his power." Schweig.

7. It has been objected to Epictetus that he expresses no sympathy with those who suffer sorrow. But here he tells you to show sympathy, a thing which comforts most people. But it would be contrary to his teaching, if he told you to suffer mentally with another.

8. "If I yet pleased men, I should not be the servant of Christ," Gal. i. 10. Mrs. Carter.

9. The sixth part of a drachma.

10. This passage is explained in the commentary of Simplicius (xxxiv., in Schweig.'s ed. xxvii. p. 264), and Schweighaeuser agrees with the explanation, which is this: Nothing in the world (universe) can exist or be done (happen) which in its proper sense, in itself and in its nature is bad; for everything is and is done by the wisdom and will of God and for the purpose which he intended: but to miss a mark is to fail in an intention; and as a man does not set up a mark, or does not form a purpose for the purpose of missing the mark or the purpose, so it is absurd (inconsistent) to say that God has a purpose or design, and that he purposed or designed anything which in itself and in its nature is bad. The commentary of Simplicius is worth reading. But how many will read it? Perhaps one in a million.

11. "Compare iii. 15, from which all this passage has been transferred to the Encheiridion by the copyists." Upton.

12. "It is plain enough that the philosopher does not say this, that the reckoning of our private advantage ought to be the sole origin and foundation of piety toward God." Schweig., and he proceeds to explain the sentence, which at first appears rather obscure. Perhaps Arrian intends to say that the feeling of piety coincides with the opinion of the useful, the profitable; and that the man who takes care to desire as he ought to do and to avoid as he ought to do, thus also cares after piety, and so he will secure his interest (the profitable) and he will not be discontented.

13. To admire is contrary to the precept of Epictetus; i. 29, ii. 6, iii. 20. Upton.

14. Such recitations were common at Rome, when authors read their works and invited persons to attend. These recitations are often mentioned in the letters of the younger Pliny. See Epictetus, iii. 23.

15. Fourteen was considered the age of puberty in Roman males, but in females the age of twelve (Justin. Inst. I. tit. 22). Compare Gaius, i. 196.

16. Mrs. Carter translates this, "Unless you perfectly understand the principle [from which any one acts]."

17. This may mean, "what is proposed to you by philosophers," and especially in this little book. Schweighaeuser thinks that it may mean "what you have proposed to yourself": but he is inclined to understand it simply, "what is proposed above, or taught above."

18. The first two verses are by the Stoic Cleanthes, the pupil of Zeno, and the teacher of Chrysippus. He was a native of Assus in Mysia; and Simplicius, who wrote his commentary on the Encheiridion in the sixth century,

CE, saw even at this late period in Assus a beautiful statue of Cleanthes erected by a decree of the Roman senate in honor of this excellent man.

19. The two second verses are from a play of Euripides, a writer who has supplied more verses for quotation than any ancient tragedian.

20. The third quotation is from the Criton of Plato. Socrates is the speaker. The last part is from the Apology of Plato, and Socrates is also the speaker. The words "and the third also," Schweighaeuser says, have been introduced from the commentary of Simplicius. Simplicius concludes his commentary thus: Epictetus connects the end with the beginning, which reminds us of what was said in the beginning, that the man who places the good and the evil among the things which are in our power, and not in externals, will neither be compelled by any man nor ever injured.

21. "He does not say this 'that it is bad if a man by money should redeem himself from bonds,' but he means that 'even a bad man, if he has money, can redeem himself from the bonds of the body and so secure his liberty.'" Schweig.

22. "How hardly shall they that have riches enter the kingdom of God." Mark x. 23 (Mrs. Carter). This expression in Mark sets forth the danger of riches, a fact which all men know who use their observation. In the next verse the truth is expressed in this form, "How hard it is for them that trust in riches to enter into the kingdom of God." The Stoics viewed wealth as among the things which are indifferent, neither good nor bad.

23. The other member of the comparison has been omitted by some accident in the MSS. Wolf in his Latin version supplied by conjecture the omission in this manner: "ita neque in terris divitiæ tibi expetendæ sunt." Schweig.

24. To some persons the comparison will not seem apt. Also the notion that every man should be taught to rise above the condition in which he is born is, in the opinion of some persons, a better teaching. I think that it is not. Few persons have the talents and the character which enable them to rise from a low condition; and the proper lesson for them is to stay in the condition in which they are born and to be content with it. Those who have the power of rising from a low condition will rise whether they are advised to attempt it or not: and generally they will not be able to rise without doing something useful to society. Those who have ability sufficient to raise themselves from a low estate, and at the same time to do it to the damage of society, are perhaps only few, but certainly there are such persons. They rise by ability, by the use of fraud, by bad means almost innumerable. They gain wealth, they fill high places, they disturb society, they are plagues and pests, and the world looks on sometimes with stupid admiration until death removes the dazzling and deceitful image, and honest men breathe freely again. In the Church of England Catechism there are two answers to two questions, one on our duty to God, the other on our duty to our neighbor. Both the answers would be accepted by Epictetus, except such few words as were not applicable to the circumstances of his age. The second answer ends

with the words "to learn and labor to get mine own living and to do my duty in that state of life unto which it shall please God to call me."

25. Mrs. Carter says, "I have not translated this fragment, because I do not understand it." Schweighaeuser says also that he does not understand it. I have given what may be the meaning; but it is not an exact translation, which in the present state of the text is not possible.

26. This fragment is perhaps more corrupt than XXIX.

27. I am not sure about the exact meaning of the conclusion.

28. This is not a translation of the conclusion. Perhaps it is something like the meaning.

29. This is not clear.

30. It is observed that the term "just" applies to Aristides; the term "god" was given to Lycurgus by the Pythia or Delphic oracle; the name "savior" by his own citizens to Epaminondas.

31. Schweig. quotes Polybius ix. 10, 1, "a city is not adorned by external things, but by the virtue of those who dwell in it."

32. Compare lviii.

33. Pittacus was one of the seven wise men, as they are named. Some authorities state that he lived in the seventh century BCE. By this maxim he anticipated one of the Christian doctrines by six centuries.

34. The marbles of Carystus in Eubœa and the marbles of Tænarum near Sparta were used by the Romans, and perhaps by the Greeks also, for architectural decoration.

35. This fragment contains a lesson for the administration of a state. The good must be protected, and the bad must be improved by discipline and punishment.

36. Compare Xenophon, Memorab. i. 4, 17. The body is here, and elsewhere in Epictetus, considered as an instrument, which another uses who is not the body; and that which so uses the body must be something which is capable of using the body and a power which possesses what we name intelligence and consciousness. Our bodies, as Bishop Butler says, are what we name matter, and differ from other matter only in being more closely connected with us than other matter. It would be easy to pass from these notions to the notion that this intelligence and power, or to use a common word, the soul, is something which exists independent of the body, though we only know the soul while it acts within and on the body, and by the body.

37. This bag is the body, or that part of it which holds the food which is taken into the mouth.

38. Mrs. Carter in her notes often refers to the Christian precepts, but she says nothing here. The fragment is not from Epictetus: but, whether the story is true or not, it is an example of the behavior of a wise and good man.

39. This is the doctrine of God being in man.

40. This fragment is not from Epictetus.

41. The meaning of the second part is confused and uncertain.

42. This is a valuable fragment, and I think, a genuine fragment of Epictetus. There is plainly a defect in the text, which Schweighaeuser has judiciously supplied.